Love and Poetry

Written by: Birdie Jean

<u>Introduction</u>

I don't know when I fell in love with love. When the only thing that mattered to me was becoming someone's wife. No matter who I loved, they always got all of me, everytime. I made sure to give every ounce of myself, to go above and beyond so that they would never feel how I felt in love, unloved. I made sure to cross all of my T's and dot all of my I's when I gave my love to someone. I never wanted anyone to tell me that I wasn't good to them. That I didn't love them enough or I didn't appreciate them.

I do know that, love for me started at a very young age. I was 5 and my family lived in Ohio. There was a boy named Ben and my five year old self LOVED Ben, I mean, really loved him. I took care of him when he fell out of the tree, I got him bandaids. I was on his team during a scavenger hunt (because his mom knew how much I loved him) and we won. We shared a milkshake and watched movies. He walked me home and he sat and talked to me, still to this day, I remember what Ben was wearing; red mesh shorts and a white t-shirt.

That wasn't "puppy love", that love taught me something about myself, something that I wouldn't realize was so important until later in my life, at this very moment. When I began to reflect and question myself about my love.

That love was pure, that love couldn't be touched. I carried that love with me throughout my life for a long time. Looking back, as I am much older than 5, my love, not so pure and some would say just a little cold. I have to retract my falls to get back to that pureness or, at least find where I lost it.

<u>ARTIST</u>

My parents were artists

They painted me a fairytale

And a nightmare

The kind the movies never show

The kind that the only ones who know-

Are the ones who live within the four walls

And a roof

Of the living hell

Painted to look like heaven

The demons of their story haunt me

Falling in love fast

Got me -

Wrapped, chained and my mouth covered

With country chrome

Walking in their footsteps

No one to save me

Eyes open to watch as they taught

What love was

Growth meant- eyes shut

Couldn't witness

What their love was

Self taught what love was

To me-

Wanting anything but their fairytale

I just couldn't run fast enough

Out of the way of their makeshift love

Following his and her

Footsteps

Love overnight

But- knowing

A foundation is what needs to be

That's my fathers' side of me

My mother-

Is she strong or weak

Questions left unanswered

And I am left searching

For the answers inside of me

Looking what your love did to you

As her blood runs through my veins, too

Don't know what to choose

The fairytale or -

The nightmare

<u>MURDER I SAW</u>

I've witnessed

Countless murders

I know the killer

I know the victim

I hid the weapon

Year after year

Time after time

He's been caught

But,

The justice system of love

Sets him free

Each and every time-

The glove fit

And that wounded me

Punctured my heart

Where love slowly spilled about

Tears rolling down her face

And that ruined me

Overflowing thoughts

A lot like my mother

I was strong in the wrong way

Much like my mother- I-

Stayed in situations - where

Love was a facade

And sex and time spent

Was a manipulation

To what love really was

Alive in the flesh

Dead in the soul

The killer still has control

<u>ABOUT LOVE</u>

I use to say

"Not everything is going to be

Peaches and flowers"

It use to be my favorite line

At some point I knew we would erupt like a volcano

And I was okay with that

My heart said

"it's okay to

Swim in the fire-

If you feel the pain

at least you will know you're alive"

With my whole heart-

I used to believe that

But,

Now I know,

Everything can be

Beautiful blooms

And of the juiciest fruit

Now,

I don't make the correlation between

The heart

And love-

Thats made up

The heart knows nothing of love

But our souls,

Our souls feel every ounce of everything

I believe we create our own wounds

For- I've had to stitch

And restitch

Myself a million times

Over things my mind devoured before -

My soul spoke

People say:

"If you aren't fighting-

You aren't really loving each other"

I lose my mind over that

That's a self inflicted wound

And the blood is dying to leak

And cause a mess

That will always remain

For-

Blood stains never really go away

The scars might fade

One day

But all it takes is

The same scent

From that day-

And you see the fresh blood

Hit the white carpet

Like it was earlier that day

I believe in all things perfect

When people hear me speak that

I see naive written on their tongue

Before they open their mouth

I admit, I haven't gotten it figured out

But

I just know-

Love isn't a fight

<u>NEVER DYING</u>

Forever safe with me

You will live forever

I write the stories of our lack of love

And how they treated me fallacious

Their names now metaphors

And titles become the days I once adored

And the nights that I lived for

They don't even know

Because they don't know-

I write poetry

Because

I never made them listen

To the words that came out of my mouth

A drought within my own brain

Something should've clicked

But it never did

I remained oblivious and innocent

A naive heart- I refused to admit it

I am infamous for making old flames

Live forever

I never intend to pen out a bad day

I just intend to keep my promise

To keep them safe, forever

For the flames live forever

I turn them into poetry

<u>UNTITLED</u>

I don't ever want to be in love

Being in love brings comfortability

I don't want to be comfortable

Just sure

I want to continuously be falling

Being in love becomes stagnant

Of course-

Problems and babies are born

And that will nudge the edge of monotony

And rock the foundation of repetition

That love has found

That will make you feel again

But that does not feel like falling

Just keep me falling

<u>IF I</u>

If I were a maker of things

Id make all of your worries disappear

If I were a painter

I would paint Zeppy near

If I were a healer

Id heal your broken heart

But

I got bad news, baby

I'm not any of those things

But, I got good news too

I'll be here to hold you

When your world is falling down

When it becomes too heavy

I'll be there to pick it up

I won't leave until-

Every star in the sky

Burns out

I promise to lie awake in silence

If that's what you need

You can lean on me

FIRE LOVIN'

Wick dipped

Splish splash

Goes the-

Wax

Hit the hide

Burning

Never felt so good

Searching for a burnout

No time soon

Flower pedals

A flame bloomed

More than a fire

Whatever the body desires

No satire

<u>BREAKFAST</u>

He didn't need a recipe book

He knew how many-

Strokes of the whisk it took-

To- scramble my eggs

And toast my buns

For breakfast

He busted right on my melons

And drank my juices

Fresh from my fountain

It must of been broken

For- it wouldn't

Stop gushin'

He was the best cook

<u>LOVE LIKE RAIN</u>

My love for you is much like the rain

No matter how soft it falls

You'll always feel it

<u>THINKING OF ME</u>

When you see the sunrise-

I hope you think of me

I hope I cross your mind

Like a shooting star

Crosses a midnight sky

When you hear the rain coming down on your roof

I hope you hear nature calling out my name

Come back to me like the dark comes to day

tonight , I had a moment of weakness

I looked at the cloud covered moon

And I seen a movie of love-

About

You and me

I couldn't help but wonder

Do I ever cross your mind

Like a shooting star crosses a midnight sky

Have you ever cried a tear over leaving me

I hope you think of me like-

I think of you

Like the moon sets and the sun rises

Come back to me

Like the day comes to dark

<u>CRAZY GIRL</u>

They call you crazy for loving more

Than you'll ever be loved back

That's not just any kind of crazy

That's crazy strength

Crazy courage

Crazy brave

And if you love the ones who

Call you crazy for loving

"Too much"

Maybe you are their kind of crazy

Because they don't deserve your love

Or maybe

They do

Because maybe they've never

Felt a genuine hard and fragile love

And you know

Your love can change the world

That's why you're crazy

POEM ABOUT LOVE

When I write a poem about love or anything, really

I see you in my head

A movie begins to play

And when the pen stops

That's when the forever is made

ALL GREAT THINGS LEAVE TOGETHER

I aint seen a sunrise

And I aint seen a shooting star

since you been gone

It's not what you wear

It's not us

And it took me a long time to figure that out

I blamed myself

I thought for days about ways

I could have prevented his mistake

Eventually- by that time

I was forced to accept and apology

I'll never get

I had to forgive him

That was the only way I could forgive myself

For letting something like that happen to me

For not being strong enough to fight him

For my NO not being good enough

That night-

I lost my ability to say no - anymore

To say anything at all to anyone

I lost confidence in myself

I became insecure

I lost all my security I had in the world

For anyone

I became angry and reckless

I was stolen

Every part of me

And I still have yet to get

Even half of me back

I don't get to be who I coulda been

Because of him

Is this me better than who I woulda been

If he didnt take that me away

Questions without answers

That haunt me every day

<u>SAVE YOU</u>

Take off your mask

Let your tears build me a river

And I'll swim to your rescue

Tell me how to save you

Mouth to mouth - won't do

A heart to heart-

That's a break through

Trust me

Take off your mask

Show me the real you

Let your tears build an ocean

And I'll swim to your rescue

<u>BILLION ROSES</u>

I could bathe in a billion roses

For a billion years

And your scent would still rest upon

My smoothed freckled skin

Just one touch of your lips upon mine

And my mind wanders

To a billion years from now

Our ghosts' shadows making love -

On the edge of the forever- we always wanted to see

You, too scared to open your eyes

To see forever through

And me, too strong to hold on

A billion years later

Your scent still lingers

And, a billion roses rest upon a grave

Not mine

Not yours

But

Our forever

Still lingers on

Our ghosts shadows

Making love at the edge of our never forever

From a billion years ago

Forever

<u>LOVE LIKE</u>

Words like

I love you

Touches like

I love you

Words like

You are the most beautiful woman on earth

Touches like

I want to marry you

Words like

Be my girl

Touches like

Our baby will be born in love

You left my vagina

Not like you found it

Words like

trichomonas

And you have the nerve to trip on me

For popping up

Where you touched me like

You were safe

Words like trust

Broken

Touches like

Windows should shatter

Where was the condom wrapper

Words like

Naive

I was

When you said words like

I love you

And touches like

You were at the end of your search

I look at you in your face, hurt

And you smirk

Words like

I'm sorry

I didn't know

Touches like

Wiping my tears away

And I don't jerk

Words

Like

I forgive you

<u>DREAM SELLER</u>

Dream seller

Dream seller

You let me purchase with my heart of gold

You're a dream seller

Your words came crashing down like

9/11

Actions aint make a sound

Dream seller

I bought the crown and it fit

I looked really, really pretty

But, you aint have a throne for me

You're a dream seller

Dream seller

Why would you want to hurt me

Why would you- why would you

Let me purchase with my heart of gold

It's not worth nothing

If it's not inside of me

You're a dream seller -

Heart collector

Your words fell flat

And I fell for em'

I purchased em'

You're a dream seller

Locked me in a cellar

And threw away the key-

To your heart

You're a dream seller

Wake me up

From this nightmare

Mr. Dream seller

<u>RUNAWAY</u>

She paints her eyes and lips

Dresses in something killer

She's runway ready

I mean

Run away ready

She plays that trap rap

To keep her mind steady

Trying to derail the thought of killing herself

She knows this feeling all too well

It takes everything in her -

To climb out of bed

To get that check

Monday through friday

She's through before the week even starts

Alcohol and drugs aren't her forte

She has nothing to turn to

Nothing to numb the pain she's going through

She holds it all in

She's too emotional

They told her

Picture perfect

She's smiling

But her soul is heavy

She hugs them tight

Hoping they'll feel her heartbeat

Hoping they might ask

Is she alright

She's left in her bed

Tossing and turning at midnight

She might be too good for them

But she's never good enough for her

She's at war with herself

Bang

Bang

Thoughts to herself

<u>SEXUALLY FREE</u>

I've never been able to

Roll over and-

Pleasure him

Without wondering

Who was before me

And who will be tasting my treasure

Left over

I've never had anyone

For only me

I've never been able to explore

My-

Maybe- wild side

That's dying to come alive

I've been limited to

On top

Back seats and

Backshots

Never been able to be wide open

Sexually free

I've been sexually free

He took sex from me

I've never been comfortable enough

To enjoy

Someone pleasuring me

Never been able to relax

Constant thoughts like

What do you think of me

Is it good to you

Is my stomach flat enough

I don't know if it's good to me

Physically, I felt the rush

But-

It's more to it than that I'm sure

Situationships

Stick to the script

Show me how loyal you can be

Real screams

I've never let out

Dreams

Of my body being spread about

Opaque

Do you see me now

<u>SITUATIONS</u>

I'm in a situation

And I love him

And

He loves me

But- he aint with me

But- when we're together

He tells me his dreams

And I believe in them

And I believe him when he says

I'm where he wants to be

I feel him when he says

Don't you think I wanna see you too

Don't you think I wanna wake up next to you

Have coffee with you

Spend my life with you

Die before you

So

I don't have to live without you

What do I do

When did I go from reality to dreams

I'm so confused

Because

If the tables were turned

And I was him

And he was me

And we loved each other

Like we do

I'd do everything I could to be next to him

I'd leave who I had to leave

To be with him

If I had it my way

No one would be in the way

Love would have its way

Of

Turning dreams to reality

Do I let go of love or-

Do I hold on

And let it playout

Will there be consequences

To our love

Will karma catch us

If true love is involved

Because

When he holds my hand

I tremble

When he kisses me

I see the white dress and black tux

I'm in a situation- I'm kind of stuck

And I don't know what to do

Do I stay in my dreams

Or let reality have its way

I'm in a situation and I-

Don't wanna let go

I wanna let love grow

He says he's in a situation

He don't wanna be in

But he can't let go

Because, his situation is bigger than us

We are in a situation

Is it love or

Is it really lust

I felt the strokes and the thrusts

The kisses on my neck

His grip getting tighter and tighter around my neck

My body felt it all

My body was fully aware that sex was taking place

My mind wasn't present

And the tears were racing down my face

As I stared into the abyss of-

His dark brown eyes

Soul scared

I was hiding

And he was whispering

Baby

Baby

Baby

In my ear

He turned me over on my back

Not missing a stroke or a thrust

Arms strung messily about his neck

I felt my body getting hotter and hotter

And I exploded

Without feeling a thing

My soul was gone

It was just my body

And he didn't miss a stroke

Or a thrust

Or me

He just wanted my body

FOOLS GOLD

He was fools gold

And I was his fool

I heard his harrowing cries

I believed all of his manipulating lies

I should've known

He looked me in my eyes but

His

His were dead

I couldn't get past the outside

They didn't lead anywhere

Anywhere I should've gone

But I went anyways

They shined in the sunlight

And glistened in the water

His words worked like magic

I love you

Melo-dramatic

He is still not what he seems

He is not his lies

<u>BLAME ME</u>

I run to wash my saturated body

Of the smell of lust and facades

Our souls left a flood our bodys

Couldn't handle

The signs I'd negate

Put all the blame on me

I'll just call it self-hate

You told me in so little words

Different years

Different months

Different times

Same line

it 'll never be

You and I

WISHING WELL

Wishing well

I'll feed you all the coins I've ever seen

Answer my one wish-

Make me his queen

SIX FEET

I love him

From the top of his head

To the tip of his toes

That's six feet and some

Of love

And - everyone knows

Six feets means your heart doesn't beat

Bury me today- because

Every time he looks at me

I see heaven

When he touches me

I am in heaven

Can you imagine if he kissed me

With his soft pink lips

Surrounded by a beautiful black mustache and beard

That would put the nail in my coffin

His caramel skin melting on top of me

You cant see where the two meet

My heartbeat stopped

Give me my six feet

<u>UNTITLED</u>

I bought real tickets to a fake show

Sold my soul to a sell out

You sold me a rent to own dream

And I was paying rent

And you were the landlord

Reaping the benefits

Broken sinks

Not fixing shit

Called on you

And voicemail

Was the only voice I heard

You got what you wanted and split

See me once a month

At your own convenience

I play along and let you inside

You're expensive as shit

I threw my pride out the window

And yelled

Take me on a ride

I didn't care what it cost

Everything lost could never be gotten again

Until we meet again

<u>WHITE DEVIL</u>

Dancing with the *white* devil

Scootin and pushin

Hes on fire

His power takes me higher

I don't know when we met

When he first took my breath

When we kiss

His power goes straight to my veins

Heart beating out of my chest

Divest myself of my own thoughts

Dressed in crystals

White devil

Smokin hot

Fallin in love

In the front seat

I end up in the back

When the *white* devil disappears

I still feel his existence

He lets it be clear

We ain't done dancing

Our dances are private

We get nasty

No one can stand to watch

The devil and I dance

<u>PARALYZED</u>

He's every drug I've never done

Marijuana only gets you so high

I ain't been marijuana high since

Twenty twelve

Here I am staying up 40 hours at a time

I guess falling back into love

Makes you blind

I guess it makes sense

Because

Your heart remembers the heartbreak

And the time that it took to recover

Your heart is screaming

No

As you lift one foot off the edge to

Try and fly with love

Your soul whispers

Heart- it's too late

She already fell

Hold on tight

It's about to get bad

Get the bandages and liquor

She wants it too bad

Those green eyes leave her breathless

Memories formed a minute ago

Leave her paralyzed

He's her doctor

He prescribed the lies

Her heart lies in his hands

This heartbreak is gonna leave her to die

And the skies to catch her shadow and devour her

He showers her with time

When she's with him

There's no time

Only time there is-

Is when it's time for him to go

Then she's watching the clock

Hoping he comes around again

She knows he's no good for her soul

He even told her so

I guess that's why

She holds so tight

She knows what goes up has to come down

Taking flight-

She's not scared to hit the ground

I know- thats what every drug I've never taken does

<u>LOVE, LOVE ME</u>

Why does love not love me

All the time I've put in

Blood into love

That just don't love me

Tears into love

That just don't love me

Am I not pretty enough for love

Love, just love me

Maybe it is my love

That love is scared of

It is strong like a wild horse

But soft like a distant mist

That will leave you soaked

To the bone

Not a years worth of sunshine

Could you be dried by

Maybe, my love

Love has dreamed of

Much like myself

Dreaming of a love

Like the love I love

<u>HURRICANE</u>

Just like a hurricane

I come and ruin the memories

You use to love

And leave

That's what hurricanes do

Its just in my nature

<u>I'M NOT BLUE</u>

My brown eyes will never shine blue

My dark locks will never show blonde roots

Our memories won't outlast

The love of you two

Too fast I grew attached to you

Hundreds of untold truths

Seduced

With laughs and memories from the past

And instantaneous transmission

Trying to make it last

She will never be

A brown eyed freckle faced

Beauty- who is me

And I'll never be your blue eye'd flame

That can never be extinguished

Pretty brown eyes just don't shine blue

Pretty brown eyes just aren't for you

HORIZONS OF HEARTBREAK

Form the wooded love

You see through the spaces in the shrubs

A long line

Power lines and pipelines

White lines

Gone in a second

You see love in the distance

Simply

Non-existent

A mirage on the horizons of heartbreak

<u>BREAK</u>

I want to break

every radio

I want to break

every bottle of Tennessee whiskey

I want to break every

Taylor guitar

Every picture on the wall

Burn every Nashville bar

Rebuild the wall we broke

I want to kill

Jack and diane

I knew better

Love only comes back around

On a big screen- not in a small town

I was Belle and he was the Beast

Plot twist

There's no dance and he doesnt turn into the prince

He left his hand prints all over my soul

With whispers and words he never meant

I want to break

Everything that smells like a memory

Every Joop bottle

Can go straight to hell

He's breaking my heart

Subtly

No harsh words

Sweet ones, really

No goodbye

Just conversational memoirs

That will keep me up at night

Saving me but torturing me at the same time

I broke my own heart

So he didn't have to waste his precious time

Breaking a weak heart like mine

Cause I know this is what its gonna do

Break me

GREEN EYE'D BOY

Steal beams break

Green eyes and a grin

Is all it took

An old flame burning me again

Again- I'm not a blue eye'd blonde

Somethings never change

I'm just a brown eyed girl

Wishing you'd see

I just want to love you

Somethings never change

My green eye'd boy

My eyes may not sparkle blue

But my heart sparks for you

Green eye'd boy

Why don't you love me

RICHEST WOMAN

If I died today

I'd be the richest woman

A million dollars

And all the gold in california

They'd rip my house apart

They'd think too hard

Where'd she leave her riches?

Did she burry it in the back with the dogs?

They'll dig up my grave

Searching for my riches, baby

A million dollars

And all the gold in california

But, all they'd have to do is-

Look up your name to find my riches, baby

They might be mad

When they find out

You don't have my million dollars or

All the gold in california

Because to me-

You are more than a million dollars

And all the gold in california

If I die today

I'll die the richest woman, baby

<u>UNTITLED</u>

Im a murderer

I like to feel and see

The struggle through my own tear filled eyes

The suspense is killing me

Every breath that I take next to you

Is another breath closer to my souls death

Every sleepless night

Because, I couldn't feel the beating of your heart

Against my back

But somehow I slept for days

When you went away

Every tear I let roll down my cheek

Because I couldn't be next to you

When you are present

I stay awake

Until the day breaks

I don't want to miss a minute

Because I know

When you're gone-

You're gone for good

I'll blame myself for missing something

That could've changed it all

I'd rather die a billion deaths

Than to breathe a day without you

It's a slow but steady

Sweet- sweet torture

What am I doing to myself

When I look at you

It's another breath closer

To my souls death

But I refuse to shut my eyes

I will endure all of the heartache and pain

Because you are worth

The death of my soul

I'm addicted to your presence

Just let me overdose

<u>THE REAL GOODBYE</u>

What am I gonna do

When it's the real goodbye

Will I sleep for days?

Will I cry many tears?

Will I wish death upon myself?

Will it be a heartbreak or

Will I pretend to be okay

To make myself forget it all

But when it's the real goodbye

Will you wish you had loved me

Like I loved you?

Will you wish you had one more day

When it's the real goodbye

Will you tell me

Or

When you walk out the door

Will my soul just know

<u>UNREAD LETTERS</u>

To whom it may concern-

Why don't you love me

For I have loved you since I was 17

We parted ways

One of my greatest heartbreaks

To date

I couldn't count the time

That it took

Before I could hear your name

And cry four oceans

But eventually I was okay

7 years later

Here I am

Falling back in love with you

What's it gonna take this time

I felt the steel beam

When it broke

Will you love me or let me down

Maybe a question I should ask in person

Not just write down

I had no plans of falling for you

Or even seeing you

I was fine being a friend in the distance

But you caught me

Engulfed in questions- like flames

In a burning house

Did you mean to?

Was it your intention to make me fall again

What are you plans with my heart

I know you feel the way

I feel about you

I didn't pack a parachute

I didn't plan for this

So many questions

I wanna hear your answers

And you're not the lying kind

Maybe I'll save the questions of my soul

So I'll have one more day with you

<u>DEJAVU</u>

The taste of dejavu

Strong and bitter

I've seen this

The same ending

Heartbreak

"You're too good to me"

Right before you break ties

Goodnight

Really turns into goodbye

Yeah-yeah

Yeah, this take just like dejavu

Questions like:

Why did I fall for you

Tears falling for you

Damn, am I really crying for you, again?

Feels just like dejavu

I pray to God, it aint-

Dejavu

Last time you shook me like an earthquake

I felt, my mistake

You can't tell me

You ain't feel my love

That's one thing I'm certain of

Prove me wrong

I don't want to see my first heartbreak

Double take

<u>DRUGS</u>

Im strung out

No,

No pills

No coke

No dope

And, I can't hold my liqour

Hangovers I hate em'

But I'm drunk

And strung out

How'd I come to this

Your smile

Your touch

Your laugh

Im strung out on you

I'm drunk on the memories

High on the fear of your goodbye

I can't get enough of you

A day without you

Is a living hell

The minute you're gone

I start shaking

I need my fix

If it ain't you

I don't want it

You Are good for me

You get me out

Take me high

You brought me back to life

Im strung out

I'm drunk

All on you

You're the best drug

I don't want rehab

I don't want to be sober

<u>CAPTAIN AND ORANGE JUICE</u>

Morning peeking through the old bamboo

Captain and orange juice on my breath

And you all on my skin

From the night before

Me wrapped up next to you

In the house you grew up in

Memories of back when

Visions of a future

Of forever

And this is what I see

<u>UNTITLED</u>

Her hair will never be flawless

Her mind made of velvet rose pedals covered in thorns

Eyes probably a little too sad

She's in love with flying at night

Just to see the runway lights

And landing in big cities

Just to see the city lights

Only to run from the city- to where

There are no lights

Just to kiss the darkness

Fun to her is boring the next

Perplexed you'll be left

By-the way she loves so intense

She believes thats how its supposed to be

You're supposed to love so deeply

So deeply

You drown yourself to keep the loved afloat

Her black soul was born an angel

Yet, no one seems to understand

How many times will she drown

Before someone understands- that

You can't save someone who doesn't

Need to be saved

For God's sake, you fool-

She's an angel- with a black soul

She doesn't need you

But if she wants you

She'll drown herself to keep you afloat

Because she knows

She's an angel

And she cant hide her halo

DREAMING OF EVELYN

Whatever you did to him, dreamy eyes

Undo it

Whenever they mention your name

He doesn't see me

It's like tunnel vision hits him

And he's back in an old scene

He cant hear me

The sound of your name is much louder

Than my voice that calms his rage

Your name is stronger than hurricane winds

He won't touch me

I don't know how long it lasts

But undo it

You're not good for him

You destroy everything that's good for him

Maybe it's the memories

I've never seen you

But if I had to guess

Id say

You're a blonde with-

The bluest of yes

Sweet Evelyn, just say goodbye

<u>WHAT A MAN</u>

Oh what a man you are

The way you are able to handle me

As I lay and open my legs

You love me, like-

You are here to stay

It's a bumpy ride

But you-

You are well prepared

Lovin' the way my back side looks

When you make my hips sway

The way my body responds

The way your eyebrows lift

When I begin to spit

When the gates open

And the real flood begins

Such an impinge

The way I clench my apperception

Around how- destitute

Your eyes alter to bloodless

Unable to handle past the somatic

Oh, what a man you are

You don't heed the needs of my intellectual satisfaction

To you-

My mind is just a distraction

To your sexual attraction

Oh what a man you are

You grasp the palpable

But suck a rumination

And the rumination of your mind

That'll get me soused everytime

It's clear-

You can't handle me

When I open my mind

Oh

What a man you are

Not

<u>UNTITLED</u>

I'm a one in a billion flower

The wind blew his way

And then the wind blew again

And he ran away

He must of forgot

He had my heart in his hand

Because as I stand here I am

Heartless

But my heart still beats in his hand

He is where I long to be

Where I must belong

In the hands of a killer

I landed so gracefully

In the hands of a killer

I grew- strong

I am one in a billion flower

And no one can pick me

<u>LOVED HIM</u>

I loved him then

And I hated myself for it

After he broke my heart

I asked questions like

Why would he love me back?

Because I wasn't good enough

He deserved someone far better than myself

I love him now

And I hate myself for it

Because he broke my heart, again

And I ask myself

Why would he love me back

He deserves someone far better than myself

I'll love him til' I die

And I won't hate myself for it

because - I know

He knows

He is loved

As long as he dies loved

I can not hate myself

Because I loved him

UNTITLED

I often stare off into space

And find my place

When I have the urge to make love

It's your paint brush I want to water

It's your name I want to scream

Not when its 3 am and I'm awaken from my dream of you

After you left me

That's all I have left of you

Dreams-

and memories

And they both hurt like hell

I'll set fire to myself

If it's the only way I can hear that laugh

And see your smile

<u>GYPSY</u>

You can't keep a gypsy soul

And it's breaking my heart

<u>HIS MONSTER</u>

He loved her but he lied

To save her

From what- nobody knows

She didn't see the monster he knows

She doesn't believe in those

He knew- she knew

He was lying

But he lied anyway

She knew- he knew

That nothing could keep her away

Her love was there to stay

Near or far

She will love him

And he knows

He shouldn't have let her go

<u>DEADLY MAN</u>

He's friends with a deadly man

No knives or guns

Could kill the way that he does

He looks just like the man I love

He hides in the depth of who he doesn't want to be

Interminable thoughts

Back and forth

Who does he trust

Him or-

The man he doesn't want to be

The killer of his happiness

The ender of his forever

He goes with the killer man

And ends his love

And that's when

The killer killed him

Suicide

<u>FEAR</u>

I guess my biggest fear is-

He forgets me

The only thing I gave him was my heart

And

He gave me the world

Everytime he said my name

Everytime he touched me

Everytime he didn't say anything at all

Everytime he laughed

Everytime he smiled

Everytime he took a breath

The world compared to my heart

How could I even think he's gonna -

Remember me

<u>UNTITLED</u>

Too good to you

You think I am

No good for me

You say you are

Scared for me

You say you became

No clue I have

About who you are

Run, far you go

Little do you know

I go, wherever you go

For once you have loved me

Forever you will- carry me in your heart

<u>KILLIN HER</u>

Is it killing you that

You're killin her

Leaving her with no goodbye

Is killing her

She's fighting for you

Fight back tears for you

And you know you're killin her

Thinking you're not good for her

Leave your favors at the door

You're killin her

You were good to her

You being gone

Is doing no good to her

Sleepless nights without you

Wake up- you're killin her

<u>DARKNESS</u>

I will wait out your darkness

And then when you fade- past the darkest

I will wait for you

I don't care how long it takes

I know your light will return

And it will be my face you see

Waiting for you

And then you'll only know

Half of the love I have for you

UNTITLED

Debris of a 1,000 lovers from before

Worst case scenario

We'll burn the bridge

As we meet in the middle

And kill ourselves

Trying to love each other

UNTITLED

I could be blind

And I'd still see you

I could be deaf and still hear you saying-

I love you

For I've never seen you with my eyes

And you've never said "I love you" with your mouth

A delusional dreamer I could be

intuit - dejavu

A love lost and secluded

I still found you

<u>ANOTHER HIM</u>

It all starts with a smile and a "hey ma" or-

"Whats up redbone"

She blushes- that gets her blood flowin'

Next thing you know

Sweaty sex and loud moaning'

Ending with a blunt burning-

That gets her blood flowin'

Three days in- that's her new bae

They are in love - selling' dime bags

She's in love with a thug

Enough saved- she gets them section 8

He can't get a place- he's a felon

And he needs a place to stay

Next thing you know- curse words and petty arguments

Make up sex and a baby is made

Behind on the rent and a baby on the way

Petty arguments and fists raised

That gets her blood flowin

Knock-off mac to cover the bruises

Smiles to hide being abused

She refuses to be a stereotype

A baby daddy, livin on section 8 and food stamps

So she gotta stay

Next thing you know

The baby is born

That gets her blood flowin

More arguments occur

She cant take no more

She kicks him out

They can't see eye to eye

He's not buying' formula or pampers

She's struggling' and he's still sellin'

He stops seeing their son

That gets her blood flowin'

Next think you know-

Another him

Same pick up line-

Met him on the same bus line

Saggy pants, the newest j's and waves

That gets her blood flowin'

He throws her money

Buys her food and clothes for her baby

Sex and blunts rolled

That gets her blood flowin'

Bitches in her inbox

That gets her blood flowin'

Arguments and uppercuts to the lip

That gets her blood flowin'

Make up sex

I love you's

Dinner dates

And-

A little bit of spending money

Next thing you know

She's runnin down apartment halls

Butt naked- crying and screaming

Call the law

Broken glass and bruises

That gets her blood flowin'

I go throw his shit out

Next day he's back at her place-

That gets my blood flowin'

More bitches-

and

Drama from his baby mamas'

More bruises and wouldn't you know it

A baby on the way

And more fuckin' brusies

She's being kicked on the inside

And punched on the out

She's left cyrin while he stays out at night

She's in a love with a thug

The baby is born

That gets her blood flowin'

Months pass-

He's still cheating'

He's still sellin'

and

He's still beating' her

He gets locked up -

She swears she's done

This is her chance to run

With two babies she cant stay

Look what love has done

And wouldn't you know it

Another him

Long story short-

sex , blunts and bruises

That gets her blood flowin'

She's the new plug

He hits her

Thats gets her blood flowin'

Make up sex and more weed

Back together by the end of the week

She's drinking liquor straight

Cryin and facing' blunts

Came home to a trashed house

Everything broken

From her babies bed to mustard flung on the walls

And milk poured on their clothes

That gets her blood flowin'

She said she was done

I guess it was;

Make up sex and blunts burning'

Cause three days later

They're back together

Layin in the same bed

And wouldn't you know it

Her head busted wide open

He left her pistol whipped

That gets her blood flowin'

Stitches on her temple

And across her nose

On snapchat

Cussin' "fuck him and anyone he knows"

But we all know how that goes

The only way to stop the blood is:

Another him

<u>3 AM</u>

In the small town of Shelby, Rhode Island; there is a new cemetery being made. Three buildings, all three which were made from brick. Which would be which, no one knew. Even a local artist, Mena Kincaid, whom had lived in Shelby, all of her life had no idea about the cemetery being built.

Mena was a not so well known artist around Shelby. Although She donated her paintings to different charities that benefited sick children, battered women and at risk youth. She had no family, her parents died in a house fire when she was 7 and she has the scar over her right eye that reminds her of that everyday.

No escape route to exit through when that fire is set, over and over and over again.

One morning at 3 am when Mena couldn't sleep; she ran outside, body covered only by a black silk slip. She found herself dipping her paintbrush into a cup of 3 day old rain water, warmed by the moon but chilled by the 3 am breeze, that also blew her kinky bedtime curls across her freckled face. Eyes upon her, she felt- unaware from where the connect came from.

- CLICK.

She heard a switch. suddenly from her peripheral she was no longer
only in the moon's beams, but electricity lit a dark room and a
silhouette is all that was seen.
Strokes from her paintbrush to her canvas was all the night heard.
Eyes still upon her as the sun was set to rose.
Just like any other 3 am to sunrise:
Mena grabbed her painting and ran inside.
Hanging the wet painting to dry.
She made her way down the long hall to the washroom, where she drew
her blinds. Stepped out of her black silk slip, one long leg at a time
and turned her shower on and washed the smoke of her nightmare down
the drain.
Awaken by a knock on her door, she wraps her wet body and slinks to
the front door. Right eye closed and left looking through the peephole
and seeing no one through the peephole.
She turned and dropped her towel;
only to see a man standing there just as she heard the towel hit the
floor - he was standing there and she was standing there... naked and
alone; with a man she didn't know.

   "Hello.." she went to scream, but before she could finish he
reached his long muscular black arm out and put one finger over her
lips, to quiet her. He wasn't there to harm her. He bent down and
grabbed her damped towel, slowly standing up; admiring every inch of
art he seen. From her chipped purple toes to her day 3 stubbled

vagina, to her pierced right nipple. He was intrigued.

He covered her body with the towel. never speaking a word, handed her

a folded piece of paper and left through the front door, as if he

lived there. as if he was leaving for work. like he would be coming

back.

In shock, she closed the door after him and fell to her knees.

A few moments had passed and thoughts enslaved her mind. "Who was that

man" "how did he get in my apartment" and "what the fuck did he want"

and "who wAs that man" "who was that man"? "Was it him who was

watching me last night"

"Meet me. 7 pm, tonight at BayRidge restaurant - Levi" read the folded

paper which had been written in blank ink.

"Levi" "his name is Levi" she whispered as she picked herself up off

the floor and staggered to the kitchen to start her morning coffee.

Pacing back and forth- forth and back.

Trying to comprehend the perplexing moments before.

   Catching her breath and breathing in the aroma of her brewing

black coffee.

"Levi"

She pulled herself together and poured her coffee in her mug

Strutting to her room. Shuffling through her closet and sipping her coffee, trying to find clothes for work .

Black pants, black shirt and maroon combat boots will do.

They always do.

Racing the clock and grabbing her purse - she was out the door and on

her crotch rocket.. leaving the morning behind with The crisp 8 o

clock air hitting her face.

Menas hazel eyes scanning the scenery left to right, right to

left. Nothing she hadn't seen before. The same Houses she passes

everyday. Same route she rides everyday.

The same Three brick buildings she passes every day...

And, one long look right.. Levi -standing right there in the

parking lot.

"Now, that's new" she thought.

She snapped her head forward and her mind was enslaved again. This

time: the good kind of enslavement. She was intrigued, Mena wanted to

know about this man, who had seen her naked but had never heard him

speak.

All day at the hospital she was worthless. useless. Just dragging

ass. She couldn't stop thinking about Levi, what he sounded like, what

color was his eyes and did he smell good.

She was no longer concerned about: how he got into her apartment or

what he wanted or if he really wanted to kill her. She thought it was

kind of sexy- in a scary movie kind of way.

Watching the clock waiting for 5.

She was going to BayRidge, tonight. Somewhere she'd never been.

So while waiting for 5, she googled the menu "60 dollars for seared salmon" she accidentally shouted. "What the hell am I going to wear to a place like that?"

He didn't know it but he was already in her head. He was already winning and he hadn't even spoken a single word to her. she had only felt his breath climb her naked body.
That thought alone gave her chill bumps, again.

Five struck and she ran to her bike hopped on and fish tailed out of the parking lot. Running yellow lights, swerving in and out of traffic. She was riding like a maniac.
Passing houses she passed every day.
Same route home, just like any other day.

The same Three brick buildings she passed everyday. And one long look left- she wouldn't have made any other day. Curious she was, was Levi there again?

"Nope"

That made her more anxious. He was mysterious.
She knew nothing but "Levi" and she didn't even know if it was "levee" or "Levi". She began to question how to say his name. The thoughts were so loud she couldn't even hear the sound of her own bike.

She made it home, everything exactly how she left it. But a folded

piece of paper taped to her door.

"3 am has never been so intimate"

    That's when she knew. Levi was the eyes she felt and the silhouette

she saw. Folding the paper back up, she strutted her long legs back to

her room and fell backwards onto her bed, holding the paper to her

chest like a schoolgirl who has a crush on the star quarterback.

Watching the clock - tick. Tick. Tick

She anxiously awaited for 6:30 to show.

    She pulled her tired body from her black Satin sheets and got up

ripped herself bare of her clothes ran to the shower jumped in,

hitting all the spots that were required to smell delicious for her

"$60 salmon date".

    She picked out a sexy silk maroon dress with a slit clear up to

her thigh and a black pair of pumps to wear. She painted her eyes,

glossed her lips and let her curls fall where they may.

    "Do I show up a few minutes early? Or, is that showing too much

interest? Or, or do I show up late, or is that rude?"

"Do I bring my own money? Is he gonna pay for me?.... oh he better be

paying!...

Questions she didn't know the answer to. Questions she didn't know how to get an answer to.

Grabbing her license and leaving her money behind, she hopped on her bike and headed for BayRidge.

Passing the houses she passed every day. The same route she takes everyday. Passing the same three brick buildings, she passes every day and one look right and there the famous silhouette stood, again. "His ass better beat me there and not have me waiting." As she revved her engine and sped off. Trying to be nonchalant. Yeah right. She wanted him to know she seen him.

"You have arrived at your destination" her gps said.
"Wowww, look at these lights, this place is beautiful"
Stunned she was. It didn't take much to melt her heart. Lights are her weakness. Lights of any kind.

She walked in the restaurant alone and a little irritated because Mena didn't know what to tell this woman who was staring at her wearing a white button up and a black tie "good evening ma'am, what's the name of your party?"

"Uhmm" she began to speak but was interrupted by a grab around her waist and a whisper in her ear "Donuts"

"Donuts" she repeated back to the hostess with a smirk on her blush painted lips and a tiny tinkle her eye.

"Right this way" the hostess said as she led the two to their

cityscape view.

The two sat and talked for hours. Mena went on and on about the

view and the sunset and how the lights warmed her soul and Levi just

sat there and twisted his glass of chardonnay as he smiled "I'm

talking too much, aren't I" she asked as she chugged her jack and

coke... No no not at all, I love the sound of your voice" he said.

Mena put her head down and he reached across the table brushing her

curls back behind her ear and gently lifting her chin back up.

 And just like that: the clock struck 10:47 and she was darted off,

yelling bye.

Racing down three flights of stairs and out the beautiful French

steel doors, to her bike; she was met by Levi , "you can't just leave

like that"

Looking around, confused "how the hell did you beat me down here?"...

"nevermind, I have to go. Thank you, dinner was really great." And she

rode off into the moon and stars.

He was left mesmerized by her mysterious rude ways. Curious he got in

his car and drove home to his apartment which happened to be right

across the street from Mena, so if she was trying to run away from

him, she really couldn't. He'd be there... whether it be a silhouette

or crazily in her house, he'd be there.

When he arrived he didn't see her bike. That night Levi paced by his window back and forth. fourth and back, waiting for Mena to return. She never did. Not until the sun was set to rose- then she arrived wearing the same dress with the same jack and coke on her breath from the night before. Much to her surprise, levi, was sitting on her porch.

"You owe me an explanation. I waited up for you, I was worried" Levi said.

"I'm fine, you can go now" giving him no explanation. Which, who was he to demand an "explanation" anyway?

Levi didn't go, he was curious about this woman and he wanted answers.

She found that annoyingly sexy. She rolled her eyes and strutted those long legs inside, holding the door open for Levi to follow.

It didn't take long for the two to become one.
The two became two silhouettes
In a shared window, laid down when the sun was set to rose.

He'd leave at 4pm. She'd hop on her bike and drive past the houses she passed every day. The same route she drove everyday. Passing the same three brick buildings she passed everyday. And everyday she'd see Levi there.
One day: curiosity caught the cat. She asked "Levi, why are you always at those apartments?"

"That's my sister's apartment" he spit out with no hesitation.

She lives so close and we haven't met? I want to meet her. She said.

"Okay" he replied

she left it at that and continued to make dinner - as he wrapped his arms around her waist and began to pleasure her treasure.

The Days came and went.

One day Levi said let's go to my sisters. I have to let her dog out. She went to Florida for the weekend.

I said I wanted to meet her, not her apartment, she joked.

They got in his car and drove the little mile down the down the road to the three brick buildings, she passed everyday.

Walking up the stairs. Levi was rubbing Mena's butt kissing on her neck, while the neighbors were looking.

They didn't care who watched. They'd put on a show if given the chance. They were wild animals.

Levi opened the door "ladies first my love" and smacked her ass as she passed.

He threw her against the wall and began to choke her, and kiss her, as he slid his hand down her body she wrapped her long legs around him and he carried her to the couch and there right on his sisters couch they had the hottest sex.

Finished. He left her to get dressed alone, as he went to take a shower. They let the dog out and left. Like nothing happened, like they lived there, like they'd be back.

They spent the next three days at his sister's house. She called off work, he called off work. They watched movie after movie.

He'd leave the room when he got a call.

She never questioned anything expect, she began to be curious about the phone calls.

"Be right Back, its my sister"

Unaware of her conscious self she began Watching the clock ...25 minutes on the phone with his sister.. she thought..

"Does your sister know we are staying here?"

"Yeah, babe she knows I'm here.. I told you, I'm watching the damn dog"

Why are you always leaving when she calls?

"Why are you tripping"

She got up and went home. Mena wasn't one for arguments. She wants the truth or nothing at all.

days had passed . No text, no call she hadn't seen Levi. She drove to work passed the same houses, same route and passed the same three brick buildings and Levi was there, again.

This time he was helping his sister carry groceries to her apartment. SHe didn't stop. She thought if he wanted to talk he knew where she lives and knows how to use a phone.

Three more suns rose and set, no two silhouettes sharing a window..

On to work she rode.

She passed the same houses. Drove the same route and Levi was still

there. He had been there for two weeks, without a single call to Mena.

She had it. She made a left turn on her way home from work one day.

Which she would never would have made before.

Up the stairs and to the right... she knocked three times.

Levi answered the door "what the hell are you doing, Mena, you

can't be here" and he pushed her away from the door and back to the

stairs; nearly pushing off the damn balcony.

Mena was pissed. She knew in her soul, something just wasn't right.

She walked back down the stairs to her bike as she was about to ride

off, but she stopped. She decided she wasn't going nowhere.

She was going to wait for him to leave.

She didn't care how long she had to wait.

She was getting her explanation for who the hell he thought he was

putting his Goddamn hands on her. And what the hell is going on. And

why the hell she hadn't heard from him.

Oh, she was going to get her answer.

2.5 hours later, his ass comes out.

And she got a text that read "what the fuck, are you serious Mena"

 She laughed as she read it. He got in his little piece of shit gold car, the one with the missing hubcaps and drove off. She followed him 7 miles down the road before he decided to pull over. She hopped off her bike and sat on the hood of his car and stared off into sun that was set to set. Trying to hide the tears that was rushing her cheeks.

"Why would you do that to me. What the hell is going on Levi. Why haven't I heard from you? " she cried

"You can't just pop up at people house you don't know, Mena." He yelled from the window of his gold piece of shit car.

"It's your sister's house and You haven't been home. I was worried" she replied in a sarcastic tone.

"No, you knew what you were doing. You were trying to start shit"

"Start shit? With who? Your sister?"

At this point - Mena was completely oblivious. She really thought it was his sister's house.

"I needed some time to reflect, Mean, I had to find out what I wanted. I have to fix me, Mena... I didn't mean to hurt you, I'm sorry"

"What do you want me to do Levi?" She pleaded.

"Don't leave me Mena, be here for me. Wait for me... I'm trying"

Mena caved into those brown eyes and black arms. She was in love with him. She felt a fire hotter than one that took her parents from her when she 7.

Just like she didn't know how to let go of her nightmares of the fire, she couldn't let go of Levi, she couldn't put the fires out.

Levi and Mena drove the long way home. A way she hadn't taken in years. She was use to the mundane. Her sunsets and sun roses were the same. It was nice to see the green scenery and not house after house brick after brick.

That night, the two silhouettes shared a window, giving the moon a show; until the sun was set to rose.

The two were wrapped back up in black satin sheets.

The days began to feel good again.
Until His sister began to call again.

It was unsettling to Mena. She knew there was three and not two.

So she played along. She let him have the sun and the stars he longed

for.

She had a plan. She had to make sure Levi was at work before she

put her plan into action. So, she went to his job and had sex with

him, emotionless and unattached sex but, nonetheless it was sex. He

was there and she could now carry out her plan.

She passed the same houses. The same route and the same three brick

buildings and made one left turn.

A left turn she had come quite familiar with.

She hopped off her bike and walked up the stairs and turned to the

right. Knock. Knock. Knock

A woman came to the door. "Can I help you?"

The same woman she seen Levi help carry in groceries.

"Hi, I'm Levi's girlfriend, Mena. You must be Levi's sister"

That girl's eyes were as big as the moon.

"Excuse me?... sister? I'm Alexa- Levi's girlfriend, whom he lives

with."

Mena swallowed that with a grain of salt, she had been preparing

herself for what she already knew.

"Okay, well this is awkward for you, not me, because I figured it out
a couple days ago"

Mena, went on to drown Alexa in knowledge about Levi and herself.
About how she had spent three days laying on her couch, to giving
explicit, uncalled for details about the sex they had, on what seemed
like every inch of their little apartment. Basically, all of to which
could have just been summed up to, Levi, is a lying, cheating piece of
shit, who should die.

    Mena was dark. She liked black. And she liked to play with fire.
She wasn't scared to choke on the smoke.
    Mena gave Alexa options. Leave him or leave with him.
    Alexa is still in shock about everything. She kicks Mena out of
their apartment.
    Mena rode home, like nothing happened, as if she lived there. Like
she'd be back.
.. as she got home she was surprised to find Levi home- well at her
apartment. She got off her bike rolled her eyes. "What are you doing
here? Aren't you supposed to be at work" she said as she went and sat
on his lap.

"I missed you and wanted you" he said, right before he leaned in to
kiss her but she covered his mouth.

"I need some time to myself" she said. "I haven't painted in a long time and I need to. You have to leave, now." She demanded.

She got up and she watched him leave.
She watched him drive past the houses she passed everyday. The same route she rode everyday. And probably made a right turn into the three brick buildings, if she had to guess.
She didn't care though.
Anger fueled this fire she was feeling.

It was 3 am and all the night heard was a strike and she was no longer only in the moon's beams but from her peripherals, a match was all that was seen.

She ran into her apartment just as the sun was set to rose. She drew her blinds and stepped out of her black silk slip, into a shower and washed off the smoke of the third brick building where the graveyard was built.

<u>CITY LIGHTS</u>

Shame on me for thinkin'

You could see my candle light

Next to the colorful city lights

Shame on me for thinking'

If I showed you me-

From the inside out

That you would love a girl like me

And silly me for believing

I could lie next to you

Until we closed our eyes for the last time

Lord, have mercy on me

For loving a man that knows-

Id light his way to happiness

With someone who isn't me

Just so I could see that smile

That outshines the lights of -

Vegas

New york

And paris

Combined

Shame on me for thinkin'

We could ever be

Silly me for saying'

The universe was waiting for-

You and me

Shame on me for wanting you more

Than I wanted to breathe

Lord, have mercy on me

I'm just a girl-

I'm just a girl who believes in love

Oh, silly me

Oh shame on me

Because he's all I want

I could be blind

And still see him

I'd lose it

Id burn every town

We've been to

Oh shame on me

For thinkin'

Love was made for-

Him and me

<u>MISSION IMPOSSIBLE</u>

The stars and moon look different now

They use to be my go to

When I was feelin' down

You showed them to me

Up close and personal -

Through a telescope

I had super hope

And the airplanes flying around

Didn't care that we was on the ground

Staring up- trying not to choke

On the stardust

Trickling down upon our lust

When I look up

I can't help but frown

Thinkin back to when you were around

I was on fire

Comet

Talkin about

Apollo's and a compass rose

Let me undo your orion's belt

Literally no space between

Love

Hot like venus

You're my very own

Halley's comet

Now look at the space between us

I feel like mercury

My days just take so long

Alien, I am now

I just don't belong

My mind in the middle of the milky way

Which way did you go

Come back

Come take this pain away

For the tears you caused

Have oxidized my soul

I need your oils

Before I become a hole

It's like winter on uranus

You by far

The most favorite astronaut

To float through my galaxy

Oh my- you see

I seent stars

Oh my- you see

I felt it all

And just like challenger

We blew up before we go too far

<u>ALL OF ME</u>

The stranger that I was waiting for

That never came

But the smile that I knew

The smell

That I've smelled before

It wasn't unfamiliar

It wasn't a stranger

But someone I trusted from before

Touched

When I slapped his creeping sweaty palms

took

When I cried no

When I wiggled and clinched my knees

But he wouldn't let go

He was holding me like we were lovers

Like was going to be okay

Like I asked for this

As he slid on in

I laid there still as winter in England at

3 am

As he pushed in and pulled out

Not 3 but 7 times

Then had the nerve to take a breather on my back

As he was still limp inside of me

I rolled to the right and pushed him out of me

I got up

Put my clothes on

And he

He had the nerve to say bye to me

I couldn't cry

Who would I cry to?

Who would I of told?

He would of called me a liar

And said I was a willing participant

For he was a college graduate

A brotha of-

OMEGA PSI PHI

He would never tell a lie

And who was I?

<u>UNTITLED</u>

You'll never be her favorite picture

Even with the finest tailor

You'll never fit

There's not a manufacturer that has your part

It's all in her attic

You can't see it-

But,

She has a tattoo on ring finger, of love

She's painted a masterpiece

And it's all scribbles

But she- she can read every letter

In the madness

She can count the midnight stars at noon

She can see the sun rays at moonrise

She has no secrets

But shes the greatest mystery

She wants to know what you like in the morning

She believes in all things perfect

Her only promise is

That she'll never treat you wrong

She's weird

She keeps dead roses from old flames

Leaves from the grave of the man she would've killed you for

And that's no hyproble

She doesn't believe that she moves people like a tide

She believes that pride controls the mouth

And hinders the soul

She'll be broken

And cant hide it

But it won't change her for the worst

Just like a ship at sea

In a storm

She's all over the place

<u>WILD HORSES</u>

He never once spoke "I love you"

From his lips

But just like a wild horse caught in a thunderstorm

She felt every bit of the unspoken

She didn't need to hear the rain

She could feel the thunder

She knew

And just like wild horses

She ran with the storm

<u>UNTITLED</u>

What's felt can't be unfelt

I'm just playing with the cards I was dealt

And if I were

Evelyn de Morgan

I would paint you the perfect description of hell

They say -

Take a picture it last longer

But

I've got memories that won't burn

When the the flames catch

Only get blurry when the tears reach the flesh

Tell me-

What cloud do I catch

To reach my angels at rest

Im nothing like paradise

I'll mess your life up

Make you understand that-

Tornadoes are just to be watched-

Not ran for

This hell, you can't plan for

No matter how brave you are

You can't walk this walk

UNTITLED

A laugh

A smile

Familiarized

Buried deep within

And

Deep without

Never knowing the loss

Always knew it was you that was missing

Having knew you

Having grew to you

And familiar with losing you

And not having you

Around the way you were

Always finding a way back

No brass compass

Maybe it's the tilt of the moon

The waves in the rain puddles

Can you hear the rain muttering

The sweet pain

The memoires

Remembering the memories

The memoires

Familiarizing themselves

Remembering the sweet pain

Of how it felt

How you dove right in

More like-

Pushed

By the magnets of the world

Forced together

For our time

Our straight and round puzzle pieces

Fit together- perfectly

Still remains a mystery

Memories that should be distorted

Remains perfectly untouched

Unforgettable

Undeniable but

Still are familiar with my soul

<u>LOVE FOR YOU</u>

I got

Love for you

Drive a couple hundred miles

Just to see you

Knowing that it may never be

You and I

Baby

Just for one night

Use my soul- it's a telescope

See it through my eyes

I got

Love for you

I opened up wide

Like a woman pushing' out life

You penetrated my mind

And a bond was born

Monopolized

I was

By a man -

With a broken heart and a new frame of mind

Dime bags and nickel bitches

But that's not what gets your attention

Did I mention-

Circumvention

I got

Love for you

Swim in my falls

Feel me explode

Bend me over- make me touch my toes

Maybe a hallucination -

A nasty fantasy

Because you and I -

We've never

Nevermind

Because history don't lie

I touched you and you touched me

But

Not in the way we are touchin' today

See how we've grown

We are grown now

But I'm not what you want now

Maybe fuckin' you is the perfect circumvent

That I need

Because I never meant to impede your nights of

Henny and bitches

I just wanted madden dates and rooftops to watch the clouds

And to talk

About the complex circumstances of our generations

Lack of affection

I got

Love for you

<u>WAVES</u>

All of my life

I've only gone to my knees

Never past my waist

Never been in over my head

I've always walked around

Bearing a heavy load

Never telling a soul

I've traveled some of the biggest oceans

Made by my own tears

And nobody knows

No gas left in my tank

No drive in my transmission

No crashing waves to push me

Where I needed to go

I always just go with the flow

For waves

Just cause shipwrecks and the windows

To my soul to implode

And the real feelings to be exposed

Oh no,

Even in a little creek

I pray I make it across

Water left unaffected

By my take off and landing

I'd hate for someone to drown

For maybe-

My lack of misunderstanding

From the biggest to the littlest

I let the words take me under

I'll drown myself with the unspoken

Before I make a wave that causes the slightest dysfunction

I'll just be the ship at the bottom of the sea

That remains a mystery of how it got there

Because I'll never report that there was ever

Any storms during my travels

Nothing but smooth sailing

Will the photos and stories capture

Not over my head

Not above my waist

Just to my knees

Just enough

To give the world a taste

Of

What could happen

If the waves crashes

And the windows exploded

<u>STOLEN NIGHT</u>

Two as one

For the night

One on one

Crossed a line

Toches

And heavy breaths

Mine and yours

Yours not mine

And mine is just mine

Soft touches

And hard stares

Stole the night

Smiles in our eyes

Yours and mine

Yours not mine

And mine is just mine

Bodys together

Mine on yours

Yours on mine

Yours and mine

Yours not mine

And mine is just one

Empty conscience

Yours not mine

On this stolen night

<u>UNTITLED</u>

It feels so right it can't be wrong

If falling' is dying

Hand me the gun

I'll do it myself

It happened fast and hard

Heartbeats are intertwined

Slow

Mo'

He's all on my mind

Which way do I go

Back into a clinical depression

Id fastly sink

Id walk out of love

But

I don't know which window

Im crawled into

Oh

Hell no

I wanna go

But my feet won't move

And my lips

Continue to speak

And my heart continues to beat

Of the sound of his name

Echoes in my ear

This right here

Seems so right it can't be wrong

And if falling is dying'

I guess I'm walking in heaven

Where's my halo

Oh

Hell no

He has it in his hands

I must not go

Oh

Hell no

I gotta go

Woke up one day and-

Right out of the clear black sky

He flew

Like a raven

Into my sights

Scared, i shoulda been

But it happened so fast

I didn't even have time to blink

When I see him my heart sinks

I can't think

If falling' is dying

Hand me the gun

Pow pow

Bang bang

Lust is done

NATURE'S GRIP

He held tight to me

Like the root of a tree

Wrapped ever so tightly

Around the dirt

around the root of a tree

When he feels his grip loosening

He digs deep into his soil

The root is buried so deep

So even when he lets go-

I don't fear the wind

Our souls utter -

Lets go

And

Our bodies tend to be slow to follow

An hour feels like a lifetime

And that's fine-

Our thoughts mangled

With the natural energy that has found

Itself inside of him and I

My 3rd eye looks him dead in his soul

With a wink

And a whisper

There's no place like

Domicile

My fingers traces the veins down his arms

To become laced with his fingers

His mind is a provender

That feeds my famished sensualist soul

I have nowhere else to go

If it's not where he leads

The outside world is obsolete

It was destined for him and I to meet

<u>HEARTBREAKING</u>

Heartbreaking

Eyes still crying

Every song seems to remind me of him

There's no road we ain't touched

No time we aint spent

No feeling we ain't felt

Heartbreaking

Ain't no memory with dust on it

No mirror I aint cry into

Not a full night of sleep

Since he's been gone

Aint one pillow dry

Loud cries

No one can hear

Screaming in a room full of people

And no one looks

Invisible

Like I was to you

Heartbreaking

I knew

Your green eyes- glossy

Made me hazy

You were just loving me

While your heart was still

Breaking

While your eyes were still

Crying

Screaming and no one heard you

But me

Nobody knows it but me

The way you sang it

I shoulda known

You were just loving me

While your heart was still

SKELETONS

Invisible

Like the ghosts

That wander through the strongest walls

Skeletons of lovers that didn't last

Love fell like the caskets in the dug up grass

What's left to graps?

Love wasn't made for me

And

It surely isn't bullet proof

Let me tear apart the truth

Introduce

One mistake after another

To you

Here is the overview

To the gaping hole

Not one but two

Tattoos to cover scars from razor blades

Watch as I collate the memories

There will be no happily ever after

I thought they said-

Lighting doesn't strike the same place twice

I must be the unlucky one

Invisible to lust and love

I am the lucky one

Somebody for everyone

But my anyone's

Are skeletons

Invisible to everyone

<u>NEED YOU</u>

Perpeliars in the wind

Much like love

The perilliars need the wind

Just like the alcoholic needs his booze

I need you

Just like the hero needs his cape

I need you

Then you find-

It's not a need

But a want

And

I want you

Just like the alcoholic wants his booze

Much different I am

Than the alcoholic who gets his booze

I don't get you

DEMON CRY

I see your wings

In your fire

I see the white in your black

The angel in your demon

There's nothing you can do

That will make me fly from you

Make me forget about

The forever I see for us

The heaven I feel with you

Nothing has ever been more clear

We are just living second to second

Until I look up and see

How much more I've fallen

Until I look up and see how high

I'd have to climb to be okay

If your demons over threw me

I'll make those demons cry

<u>EXCUSES</u>

I don't need rehab

He died in my arms

I breathed into him

But it wasn't enough

My very breath wasn't enough

I feel him when I put the needle to my vein

Flashbacks

Racing through my thoughts

Right now I'm walking around

You see me

But, you don't feel me

Im screaming but, you can't heal me

I've got this corpse on my soul

More than just mine

I feel him when the heroin hits my bloodstream

That's how I know i'm still alive

If you don't want me next to him

Under the lush green grass

Keep me out of rehab

And keep the drug line open

If you want to see me

You'll have to see me high

That's when I feel alive

When I'm with him

Thats when I'm alive

And thats when I'm high

I feel him when the heroin

Hits my bloodstream

Keep me alive

<u>BRIGHT DARKNESS</u>

He's the darkness that makes the stars shine

He's the gas that makes the sun burn

He's everything that's anything

UNTITLED

She's not a monalisa or-

A painting by Michelangelo

She's been broken and-

Been down multiple of the same roads

She smiles a thousand smiles

That hides a million reasons to die

Everynight

She wants to try cocaine

And drink plenty of 100 proof whiskey

She's got a problem

They say she loves too much

They say she loves too deep

She says she doesn't love enough

She loves more than one can handle

Leaves her left

Picking up the pieces

Of nothing that's left

Somehow

With all the cracks

She stays warm

No love lost has turned her cold

She's a masterpiece of lost love

Her soul gets lost in love

And washed in heartbreak

Yet

She wakes up ready to love again

She's ruthless

Indestructible when it comes to love

But has been broken so many times

She gets no white doves

She just stays true to the way she loves

Strong as an eagle's sight

She hold tight to what might be

Lust in the beginning

Love in the middle

Left in the end

She gets back up to love again

Catch 22 wins again

LIES IN THE TRUTH

Unspoken truths

Tell a billion lies

But

The eyes tell it all

TRUE LOVE

The energy of our souls made our bodies meet

King of my temple you became

And the queen of your throne

I raised

You inside of me

As I slowly release

The look in your eyes

We were not surprised -that

True love has arrived

Deprived you was

And my soul malnourished

Your gentle touch between my trembling thighs

Opened me up and I rained down

My body cried

To catch every drop- you were there

Looking love in the eyes

The crying between my thighs

Became your very demise

You drowned

Trying to drink

The tears from between my thighs

Your lips wet

From the tears between my thighs

My lips wet

From your lips being wet

From the tears from between my thighs

You Didn't know death could be so sweet

So you chose to die a million deaths

TOUCHING ME

His love was like the sun

Sometimes it's shinned

And kissed my freckled covered skin

Sometimes he'd hide

But afraid I was not

Of the thunderstorms that would fall from his skies

For- I know his love was still shining

Just somewhere I couldn't go

I had evidence his love touched me

The way I walked

The way I smiled

The way I talked

My energy smelled of him

And for that- I too shinned like the sun

<u>WORSE THINGS IN LIFE</u>

Where I used to be

And where I want to be

Are the same place

And where I am now

Is a war zone

But I'm learning-

I could be worse off

I could have never

Laid in your love

I coul have never

Felt your fire

I could have never

Tasted your pain

I could be empty

<u>MOON AND STARS</u>

He knew I loved the moon

He knew I loved the stars

And when he went away

My whole world turned dark

He was the moon

He was the stars

<u>PERFECT SHADE</u>

When I looked in his beautiful brown eyes

All I seen was that perfect shade of green

And that's how I knew

It wasn't him

It was still you

UNTITLED

She-

Along with her car is left with the aroma of

His sweat

A shirt two days old, soaked, stil

With the aroma of -

What won't wash

From her memory

She gazes- and sees-

Dirty toes prints on her windows

The aroma of

Almost midnight

French kisses and-

Long licks

In her front seat

She left her aromas

On his lips

He tooks a sip

Came up and stole

A 3 am kiss

The night - left with the aromas of

Lust and what if's

<u>DREAM</u>

Lets drink deeply of love until the morning

Your heart is a highway to the gave

But I will not pine for you

You are but a dream

A star I can not touch

Until the galaxy is through with you

And pluto has rest upon your chest

And flowers begin to bloom from your fingertips

Then and only then-

Will I swoon

I will not pine for you

You are but a dream

Whose lips wet with lies

Upon my own

For the tingling in your own bones

You care not of mine

For I am just a wild flower in your sky of

Black roses

<u>DARIN'S TRUTH</u>

Another night has met the light

At the edge of darkness

Flowerbed watered with tears

From his sweet forever

His secret treasure

He keeps buried

Refusing to surrender

That X- that marks the spot

She is- everything greatness is made of

Mad

He is

And afraid

So he walks not near

Where his heart is buried

And another day has met the night

At edge of darkness

ROUND 15

Your name is the music to my soul

Your laugh makes my sky cry

And your voice makes my flowers bloom

Winter

Summer

Spring

And fall

From his skin he

Chocolate kisses

My french buttercream

I melt on his high peak

He breaks me down

And at the bottom we meet

For a long fire starting

Breathtaking

Leg shaking

Love making

Eye stare

His mouth says no words

But I hear his every thought

For his are the same as mine

Wrapped in

See through

White sheets is-

Where we'd rather be

Round 15

All on me

THE EXPLOITATION OF LOVE

I want to be your smoke

Your choice of high

When you're low

I wanna make you float

I want to smile

And you melt

I see the fire

But

I want to touch it

Is it real

Let me touch you

How do you feel

About me

Engulf my chest with your smoke

Leave your breath on my neck

Provoke your buried thoughts of love and forever

Exploit them all over me

REMEMBER HER

She never gets them

They get her- but

They never get her

She dont leave them

They leave her

But-

They always come back

By that time

She said to hell with them

She got her

She forgot them and remembered her

THE SIMPLE THINGS

They wants roses in an expensive vase

Sittin' on marble

She wants a wildflower

In an old soda can

It didn't matter if it was sitting on a table

Or an old pizza box

They want sexy dresses

And vip tables

She wants his shirt

And a dance around their kitchen table

After midnight

They got dollar signs and diamonds in their eyes

She's got love and loyalty one her side

They pray for him for them

She prays for him for him

He left her for them

She was boring to him

He wanted to play with all of them

He text her now and then

I love you

And i miss you

As she's dancing in her field of wildflowers

After midnight

She just wanted a wildflower

In an old soda can

She lost him

And she gained a field of wildflowers

She's so extraordinary to her

BALANCE

Love is like the wind

It can move the leaves of a tree

Be gentle and pure

Depending on the day-

It can be

Strong and ruthless

Depending on the day

When the sun isn't shining and-

When the rain is blowing sideways

You'll feel the wind

You'll see it

The wrath-

Is it love or is it power

And control

The ability to make rain -

Roll up

A flat road

Depending on the day

When the heat is stagnant

And the leaves aren't moved

You won't see it

And-

You wont feel it

Is it hate and disgust

Somethings the wind, rain and sun

Just won't discuss

Depending on the day

The trees have to wait for the wind to blow

Sometimes it's hiatus is slow to return

But the reward is sweet like honey

Depending on the day

When the rain is blown sideways

And the leaves are drowning and-

Have become numb to the wrath

The trees wait-

For- when the heat is stagnant and its leaves

Are not moving

Love is a balance

Depending on the day

UNTITLED

I gotta mean vice

I'm addicted to love

I feel the beginning

I live the in between

And write the end

Before the end

Before the in between

Right at the beginning

Men will make me rich

No wedding bells

Sex prevails

Celibacy was my heaven

Puff puff- inhale

No- in hell

I'm addicted to not taking my own advice

Love take me on a ride

Tell me the lies

Look me in my face

Tell me i'm your greatest prize

Go ahead-

Make my eyes cry

I'll write about it

Just to keep your memory alive

Because that's going to last longer than

We can, physically

You had me weak

Mentally

I knew better- he wasn't a keeper

He was a creeper

But he told me

He'd love me forever

Forever-ever

Forever is as long as we make it

it's not eternity

No warranty

No money back guarantee

No time wasted for me

I'll turn you into

Letters and words

Stanzas and take you to slams

Men will make me rich

Money back guarantee

I can count on me

I give them all of me

And still end up with all of me

In the end

<u>LOVE AND POETRY</u>

Love almost ruined my poetry

Almost no more poetry

I was choosing love over poetry

He made me choose love over poetry

Why did he make me choose love over poetry

Why did I let him-

make me choose love over poetry

I couldn't have love and poetry

Why couldn't i have love and poetry

If it wasn't him-

There was no white doves

Only shoulder shrugs and drugs rolled up

I need love and poetry

Because

I can't get poetry without love

And I can't get love without poetry

I am love and poetry

UNTITLED

I loved you so much

And you fucked me up so much

I turned you into poetry

I never wanted much

All I craved was-

Your touch

They way we made love was like poetry

The way you went down on me

It was slow

Like honey and my words flowin'

You had my juices dripping

Like

A beat dropping

Neighbors came a-knocking

You was clocking hours

Like

You was getting paid

You laid me out

Iike

poetry on a blank page

I felt you rage

You put my love in a cage

You were suppose to wear the cape

My poetry said

Come save me

But you weren't brave like me

You were the villain

Whole time-

I was trying to fight this feeling

And it didn't sink in

Until you started drilling things into my mental

Everything I did, was did wrong

My love really isn't that strong

My poetry aint like a birds song

Our love was wrong

But

I loved you so much

And you fucked me up so much

I turned you into poetry

I never wanted much

I just wanted you to love me

Like

I love poetry

Like

The way I make love to poetry

Sometimes -

It's a rushed mess all over the place

Sometimes its slow

Every letter the same size-

I take my time

Not every word rhymes

But the message is so clear

The blind could read between the lines

You put me through hell

Impaled my soul with your dagger

Your words hold weight

When you lost control

You couldn't wait to -

Call me out my name

You needed caged

your love was untamed

Like poetry to an open flame

Your name burns slow

With you I lost my glow

Worry not though-

Poetry wears the cape

It'll show me the way

My poetry is always brave

Like me-

I love poetry

It's dark and deep

More than I could ever-

Verbally speak

Thats why -

When you said

Leave

I leaped

I looked inside of me

The words you speak

They injured me

My poetry be healin me

<u>UNTITLED</u>

I always pulled in wrong

He never pulled out

I made a wrong turn and- he spazzed out

We made a baby and she make it out

I was almost in it for life

God gave me a way out

And I took it

Left and came back

Such a disappointment

He stayed smoking but I spaced

Thinking of a way out

Lies and manipulation

Tryna figure out

How I did everything wrong

And he was always right

How I hurt his feelings and I couldn't have any

Blushings emoji's

And "hey babies" from a chick named Erica

This goodbye was the omega

Flashbacks he liked it with my legs up

Fuckin- nuts

Walking on eggshells

Wondering when he would erupt again

Blame it all on me

Normalized

No apologies

Held in my cries

Passive by nature

I can't lie

Insecurities came to light

But-

I heard the wedding bells

I was preparing for a life in hell

Contemplated suicide

It looked like the only way out

Held off let it play out

He spazzed out

He called me out my name

And I was the one to blame

Luckily-

That was the last frame

That ended the game

INSECURITIES

I got made insecurities

That came from watching the way my daddy loved my momma

The house was full- but you could hear the echoes of my mommas

broken heart-beating

Never beating her- only cheatin' her

I can't be long- without your voicetone and touch

I probably wont ever belong- because

I got mad insecurities

That come from- guys, lickin' their lips while they're talking

to me

The air was filled with lots of vocabulary

When they were done with me

They would shine of my energy- and

I was left like a dark cloud

Waiting to rain down

On a flower picked but-

Left on the cold ground

I've got mad insecurities

If I let you close to me

You wont stay close to me

Because-

I got mad insecurities

You just seen my insecurities

What do you want from me

My insecurities are telling me

"Don't get attached"

I want to tell you how I feel

I want you to stay so bad

But I got mad insecurities

And when you go-

My mind flies on autopilot

Damn it

No gear shift to turn this shit off

I got mad insecurities

That take control of me

He dont love you

He just wanna fuck- no soul

All pussy

He'll never be faithful

You ain't pretty

enough

You aint smart

Enough

Your house aint big

Enough

Your car aint fast

Enough

Got damn it -

I got mad insecurities that come from

Mother fucka's

That's fucking friends married fathers-

Unfaithful ass

Motherfuckers- that couldn't get on stage in an empty room

And say their alphabet

Im tryna be alpha but-

I got mad insecurities

Can you love me through my insecurities

When im uneasy

Can you give me the security that I need

Do you got the keys to my lock

Put it in see if its a match

Put my fears to rest

Let them bitches burn

I believe you but-

My insecurities keep knocking and knocking

Don't knock me for having insecurities

Somewhere down the line

You'll feed my insecurities

You'll be a reason I have insecurities

Don't listen to me

That's just my insecurities

Tell me you got the cure

The answer

The remedy to my insecurities

Remember me when-

Things are good and my insecurities are low

For the moment

Because- that's who I want to be

I wanna believe it's only me that you're planting seeds to grow

with

But-

I've got insecurities that come from

A dude textin' me while he was having a threesome

Talkin' about-

Come make love to me

When I'm done doing these errands

Im still tryna figure out if their names were Erin

Im tryna be transparent with you

I wanna believe you when you say you are here to stay

I'm not blaming you

I'm just warning you

I got mad insecurities

<u>OKAY</u>

Its okay to let life let love end

Its okay not to be for somebody

It always took a lot out of me when-

Somebody would tell me-

I'm not their somebody

I took it personally

I took it as an attack

Like I wasn't good enough

I always fought back and begged

And cired

Love me back

My love is like crack

Let me prove to you that-

Im worth it

Give me a real shot

I always took shots

I was the chooser

Never chosen

But-

My heart was never frozen

I was born to love

Whoever-

Made for me

Not for me

That's all my soul knows

Love

In the 3rd degree

In 3d

You will feel my love

<u>PILLOW CASE</u>

Tears on the pillow case

Tryna get a lil taste of love

Closed blinds

And

You spoke my love language

Gave me all of your time

Spent all my time with you

Gave all my love to you

But i was the worst to you

I did things you can never understand

Never take back

No regrets

And I cant apologize for that

And because of that-

You can never forgive me

And that's okay-

I had to breathe again

See again

Closed blinds

Make-up my mind

I see the light

And it's not bright

Blame me

It's all my fault

That's what you say anyway

And I'm used to it

I got use to us

Let's just forget

What coulda been

We can't get that back

No matter how hard we fight

And we fight everyday

I was losing myself in you

I became afraid

Where did I go

Closed blinds

Don't know

Blurred lines

I come every time you call

I cum every time

Everytime you say it's the end

Everytime you win

Youre right and I'm wrong

I typed my wrongs on the phone and hit send

The truth better left as a lie

You can't look me in my eyes

Told me to take my own life

Behind closed blinds

Behind enemy lines

Tears on the pillow case

Just want another taste of love

Yes to no's

And nobody knows

Closed blinds

Nothing to show

But the light continues to glow

Brains blowed out-

Closed blinds

Open

Open

Open

I was hoping you could -

Open closed binds

Get the full picture-

No closed blinds

No sunshine

Nothing can grow behind-

Closed blinds

We were out of our minds

Because love felt good

physically

And emotionally

When it was good

But it was bad- behind

Closed blinds

I started drink to free my mind

Seen the blurred lines

Ignored every sign

Because love felt good

Physically and emotionally

When it was good

But there were tears on the pillow case

In most cases

I was apologizing when you were wrong

I wasn't an angel but I could admit when I wasn't right

When I did wrong

I knew all along

Closed blinds

KATE SPADE

Feeling Kate Spade-

But my scarf is black

And the thread that's holding everything

Together has become frayed

And I'm so afraid

Everyone is around but I'm so lonely

In my thoughts I'm so lonely

I'm my own secret keeper

And I'm tired of wiping my own tears

Tired of this never ending pain

When I close my eyes all I see is

My brains blown out on the wall

I'm at the edge- trying not to fall

I'm losing ground

I see everyone but no one is around

Im screaming but they don't hear a sound

Feeling kate spade but my scarf is black

My soul is cold

And my goodbye letter is long

No apologies

No regrets

Don't be vigilant

Im fine

Im fine, see

I'm smiling

I cant expound on what's going on

Just don't come to my funeral frowning

DESTINY'S CHILD

You messed around with destiny's, child

You changed your destiny

You took destiny's child

To save you

To give your life a second chance

To breathe

To see

Was this in your destiny, child

You soul was screaming

Like someone was murdering your joy

Your power

Your being

Who can say now

Destiny's child

No way, now

No weight, now

No wait, now

Its okay

You can be great now

You can feed your dreams

Your fantasy

You can breathe now

No looking over your shoulder

No more-

No more poetry

You had the power to change destiny, child

Feel the power you have

You changed your destiny, child

What's your destiny now

You gotta live for destiny's child

Make the lack of pain

The lack of emotion

Where there should be enough tears to fill the ocean

Where there is no motion

Create it

If you can change destiny, child

You can create your dreams

Live for your destiny, child

THE VISION

I can't imagine

I broke my heart the baddest

Get a bandage

I broke my heart the baddest

But I blame you

It's all on you

But the pieces of my broken heart

Are just cutting me

Cutting me deep

Got me thinkin'

I don't even wanna keep

What I wanted for so long

Take me to the cold room

Turn on the light

Look inside of me

Take it out of me

Get a bandage

Pretend it never happened

Pretend he never took me out

My happiness- doesn't matter

Because I was the happiest with you and-

I aint never have you

But I was happy

And now I feel so wrong

Guilt is weighing me down

Its turned my smile upside down

If I find a gun laying around

You'll find me laying around

Two holes

That's how bad

I can't take this heartbreak

Figner racing to the trigger

Pulled it twice

Take the pain away

No pain killers

I'll be a self killer if it means

Putting your heart back together

Why can't I feel happy

I can't see

I fucked up the vision

I was proud of me

I was happy

And everything was good for you -

As long as it was just me accepting you- living your life

Then the reality of me living my life

Started rushing you

Now it's crushing you

And it's crushing me

But this time

It can't be saved

This time

I took it too far

I fell in love with a shooting star

And I made a wish

And it came true

I get to see a forever but, its not with you

And it's killing me

That it's killing you

What am I supposed to do

Everybody's hell is made of the last thing on earth

That they want

For the rest of my life I will be living in hell-in heaven

Everybody's heaven is made of all the things they love-

I will be living in heaven - in hell

Get a bandage

How is it- I can't feel my happiness

How is it that you stole it-

You had a whole other life and you wanted mine too

And for four years, I gave it to you

How did I fuck up the vision

You had sunglasses on - you couldn't see how bright it coulda

been

I had none- staring at the sun

I seen it to the end

I fucked up the vision

Because this wasn't supposed to be the end

It's all your fault

But I'm the one that's dying

I can't live with regret

But im trying

But the thought of your broken heart is torture

I'd rather not be happy than to hear -

To hear the beating of your broken heart

And the cracking of your voice

I broke my heart the baddest

The baddest

I wanted you the baddest

I'm bleeding out-

Where's the bandage

Fuck it- nevermind it

Let me bleed out

Fade in and out

You took the glasses off

And now all of a sudden you seen the vision

It's in the rear view though

And reverse is broke

We can't go back there

My happiness is killing me

my tears are choking me

You gotta be joking me

Your happiness is what's most important to me

And you're not happy

Just find the gun for me

Let's end it for me

For you

For us

I can't take this heartbreak

I ended it for us

<u>FANTASY</u>

Touch me like you fantasized about touching me

Before

You finally touched me

Lay me down

Whisper in my ear

And tell me you want me, now

Make your touches last a lifetime

Make me remember the prints of your fingers

Leave your breath on my neck

Perplexed for weeks

A connection with a few imperfections

Tell me

Do you fantasize about me

When I'm not around

Does your hands crave

The feeling of my flesh

Lay me down

Look in my eyes

Memory refresh

Undress my worries

And kiss them goodbye

Will you be a frequenter

Make me remember your love

KINDA COLD

My heart was soft

And in my younger days- I hated it

Everybody played with it

Now they complain it's cold a bit

For the first time- I was called a bitch

And, I don't think he was playing- not even a little bit

But- I can't blame him

Made me question, do I even feel the shit anymore

Its like- I have no remorse

First I- put on a smile

Then I- close my eyes

Wish I- was by myself

Its when I'm my best- I

Don't know why

But, these days I can't cry

My feelings and my eyes are dried up

Wait, hold up

I never sold out

The old lovers of my life ain't make me cold

No one has directions

I never told a soul

No one knows

It'll- blow your mind

Take a - stroll with me

Let me- rewind the time

To time misspent

My love was heaven sent

My love was pure

Take me to- back then

When I- didn't have questions

Take me to- back then

When- the only weapon I had was my love

And that's what they were afraid of

Give me that love back

I want to be soft again

Fragile

Easy to break

But unafraid

Overly forgiving

For goodness sake-

I was innocent

I was a doctor

And my love was the prescription

They were uninsured

And I was addicted to fixin'

I thought everybody deserved a love like mine

Once in a lifetime

Love like mine

I never told a soul

What I needed

Them receiving my love was my healing

I never thought that- my heart could be cold

But -after all-

Love not reciprocated

Can make even the greatest love hard

I miss when my heart was soft

I wanna love like me again

Love make me, me again

<u>BEAT</u>

No bruises

Visually

Not a punching bag

Physically

Just verbally and mentally

Silent cries

And suicidal thoughts

Seclusion

From-

Family and friends

Causing confusion

They just don't understand

Love

And possession

I became his

Obsession

He just wanted control

I like it rough

And love was torture

Manipulation

And it was always my fault

Hyperventilation

How many times

Did I almost lose it

Calling me stupid

Being abused

I was stupid and confused

And

I chose you

Because you spoke my love language

Time spent

Back rubs

Big plans and-

Wedding bands

House hunting

Made my money but couldn't use it

Do you know

How many times I almost lost it

Because you couldn't save money to move

Used it to get high

Clueless as to how low

You made me feel

How many times I cried- on the inside

I lost myself trying to hide

I didn't want them to be right

I wanted to be wrong

Everyday a different fight

At night - silent cries

And questions like

Why

Smiles at sunrise

I prayed for better days

And nightmares you portrayed

I wasn't an angel - but-

I did my best

Everything at your request

I'm just a wild horse you can't break

Fences jumped

Whip,not long enough

My submission was pure ammunition

You pulled the trigger

But I got the death sentence

Luckily- I got out- on-

Self love and realizations

You didn't love my poetry like you should've

You listened but you didn't hear the cries

In the words I wrote

My silence was cut throat

You slipped on the blood and blamed me

And I cleaned up the mess as you smoked

Not missing a toke

I won't miss a hi

<u>HEAT EXHAUSTION</u>

The sun and its exhausted

Don't shine

No burn

Won't miss it- until

It doesn't return

Cold and-

Dark

Dearly departed

Waters parted

Parts uncharted

The sky was kind

And

When it stormed

Only mists

No thunder

Little lighting

But the skies

Would never be the same

The clouds would form thicker

But still the flowers bloomed

BUTTERFLY KISSES

If only roses could horripilate

Then And only then could I be myself

A yellow butterfly

Kissing her feet against the petals of a red rose

Wings fluttering

As the sweet nectar Slips backwards down her tongue

Warming her body

Filling her with the energy

She needs to fly

Returning

Even after the rain meets the petals of her red rose

The kisses of her feet

Cause an unprecedented

Horripilation from the giver of the nectar

Her sweet red rose

<u>WHEN I'M GONE</u>

When I'm gone do your fingers crave the feel of my flesh

When I'm gone do you hear the echoes of my breath

Does your back know the paths of my hands

When I'm gone do you wish we were face to face

Does it smell of memories from moments past

Do I linger on your mind

Do you feel me kissing you

When I'm gone do you wish I wasn't

Or- are you okay- when I'm there

And it doesn't bother you-

When I'm gone

Because you know I'm coming back

Do you miss me when I'm sitting there in silence

Do you notice when I'm present but I'm gone

Can you tell when I'm dancing in a daydream

Or, when I'm carrying the weight of the world

Do I titillate your mind

Just some questions of mine

When I'm floating in the sky

Do you wish you were the air that carries me

And the ground that catches me when I fall

Will you catch me when I fall

THE REFLECTIONS OF LOVE

You are my secret keeper

The open window

When my mind is about to explode

You're my go-to

My natural high

My smiles know no frown

You make everything seem possible

Butterflies

I feel safe when you're around

You're my natural high

Goose bumps and they don't go down

I wanna get down

With the feeling that you bring around

Your vibe

My vibe

Its a balance

With a natural upkeep

My beat- be, upbeat

My heartbeat

Beats faster

But I'm so calm

So relaxed

I can feel it in all my bones

From my head down to my toes

I let you know

I respect you

It's a revolving door

Spin-

Spin around

You're a mirror

I see myself in

You are the reflection

I want to mirror

You wear a crown

I wear a crown-

I wear a crown

You wear a crown

The reflections of love

Anything you can do I can do better

I challenge you for the better

But I am no better

I just want to be better

Let's be better together

The reflections of love

<u>REGRETTING THE CAKE I ATE</u>

Seen

Met

And conquered

Withdrew

Withdraw

Withdrawn

From the dawn

That wasn't hidden by illuminated street lights

New

Knew

Known

Wrong way

Don't enter

Dead end

One way in and one way out

The gangsters always told me-

Never enter those types of entities

Because-

It's one way in and one way out

How you get in is how you get out

But

I just couldn't do without

The look

The feel

The touch

The yearning

Was much more intense

Than the actual-

Look feel and touch

The yearning

Was enough cake

But I wanted-

The look

The feel

And the touch

And I took a bite

I haven't been skinny since

In the sense of-

Hunger for his

Look

Feel

And touch

I was left to starve

While she gets cake after cake

Granted,

He's given her multiple cavities

But she gets to taste

Me- I got a taste

I regret the cake I ate

<u>WHITE</u>

I thought cocaine was the only white thing that could ruin my

life

Boy ,was I wrong

White boy

Did me so wrong

<u>UNTITLED</u>

It could be so simple

Your hand in my hand

Why'd you have to turn my world mad

Why did you disappear

Turning my love against me

Why don't you love yourself

What in your history has told you- that

You aren't good enough

<u>AIDS</u>

Unbothered by the thoughts of what might happen

I dove headfirst into his aids

With open wounds of my own

The absorption of his aids

Scarred my open wounds

He thought his aids would be detrimental

But it taught me things

I wanted to feel what he felt

He was strong

But his weakness I'd become

Too powerful my love was to him

Slowly curing his aids

Exceeding his medication of alcohol and one hitters

Clear eyes and happy smiles

False realizations became his and our demise

Still alive I am

Carrying his aids inside

Keeping the hope alive

That-

Maybe one day-

He'll open his eyes
True love never dies

<u>LOST LOVERS</u>

I've lost two lovers to bullets

And I've lost a lover to love

And to be honest

The loss of two lovers to bullets was much easier than-

Losing a lover to love

For- the two lost lovers to bullets

I know where they are

I know what they are doing

And the lost lover to love

I don't know where he is

I don't know what he's doing

I don't know if he thinks about coming back

To lose the living

Is a living hell

<u>P.E</u>

I wanna suck your juices

The power which can't be uprooted

You give me a taste

Everytime we are groovin'

I take it-

You juices open me up

Your rocket takes me to a new universe

I immerse myself in your ambience

Your brilliancy- fertilizes my desires

And a new horizon blooms

Inside my minds womb

Slip and slide

Unzip- your mind

Go deeper - don't stop

Until I peek

And cross examine

All on your sheets-

Of research

Preserve

The rest

For the next time

You pleasure my mind